Calcium

and the Alkaline Earth Metals

THE PERIODIC TABLE

Nigel Saunders

Customer Service 888-454-2279

Visit our website at www.heinemannlibrary.com

Design: David Poole and Tinstar Design Limited
     (www.tinstar.co.uk)
Illustrations: Geoff Ward and Paul Fellows
Picture Research: Rosie Garai
Originated by Blenheim Colour Ltd.
Printed in China by South China Printing Company

07 06 05 04 03
10 9 8 7 6 5 4 3 2 1

**Library of Congress Cataloging-in-Publication
Data**

Saunders, N. (Nigel)
  Calcium and the alkaline earth metals / Nigel
Saunders.
        p. cm. -- (The periodic table)
Summary: Provides an overview of the periodic
table, particularly
calcium and the alkaline earth metals, describing
where these elements
are found, how their atomic number is assigned,
and uses for each
element.
Includes bibliographical references and index.
  ISBN 1-40340-872-6 (HC), 1-40343-515-4
(Pbk.)
  1. Calcium--Juvenile literature. 2. Alkaline earth
metals--Juvenile
literature. [1. Calcium. 2. Metals. 3. Chemical
elements.] I. Title.
II. Series.
  QD181.C2 S28 2003
  546'.38--dc21
                      2002152858

Acknowledgments
The author and publishers are grateful to the
following for permission to reproduce copyright
material:

p. 4 G. Bell/Zefa; pp. 8, 39 Amy Neunsinger/Getty
Images; p. 10 Jeffrey L Rotman/Corbis; p. 13 David
Taylor/Science Photo Library; p. 15 top Andrew
Lambert/Science Photo Library; p. 15 bottom
Andrew Lambert/Trip; p. 19 Archivo
Iconografico/Corbis; p. 20 Roberto de
Gulielmo/Science Photo Library; p. 23 George
Hall/Corbis; p. 24 George Bernard/Science Photo
Library; pp. 27, 28 Paul A Souders/Corbis; pp. 29,
33 Trevor Clifford/Science Photo Library; p. 30 Dr.
Tim Evans/Science Photo Library; p. 32 Lester V.
Bergman/Corbis; p. 34 T C Middleton/Oxford
Scientific Films; pp. 35, 47 Yang Liu/Corbis; p. 37
top Adam Hart Davis/Science Photo Library; p. 37
bottom Jerry Schad/Science Photo Library; p. 38
Peter Morris; p. 40 H Rogers/Trip; p. 41 Biophoto
Associates/Science Photo Library; p. 42 Andrew
Lambert/Trip; p. 44 J. Wender/Trip; p. 45 Ecoscene;
p. 46 Martin Land/Science Photo Library; p. 50 E.R.
Degginger/Science Photo Library; p. 51 Michael
Nicholson/Corbis; pp. 53, 55 J C Revy/Science
Photo Library; p. 54 Hulton Archive; p. 57 Science
Photo Library.

Cover photograph of chalk, reproduced with
permission of Photodisc.

Special thanks to Theodore Dolter for his review of
this book.

The publishers would like to thank Alexandra
Clayton for her assistance in the preparation
of this book.

Every effort has been made to contact copyright
holders of any material reproduced in this book.
Any omissions will be rectified in subsequent
printings if notice is given to the publishers.

Disclaimer
All the Internet addresses (URLs) given in this book were
valid at the time of going to press. However, due to the
dynamic nature of the Internet, some addresses may have
changed, or sites may have ceased to exist since
publication. While the author and publishers regret any
inconvenience this may cause readers, no responsibility
for any such changes can be accepted by either the
author or the publishers.

Words appearing in bold, **like this,** are
explained in the Glossary.

Contents

CHAPTER 1

Elements and Atomic Structure

We are surrounded by different substances. All around us are metals, plastics, water, and lots of other solids and liquids. There are gases in the air, too, although you cannot see them. There are also many other gases. Amazingly, over 19 million different substances have been discovered, named, and cataloged. Around 4,000 substances are added to the list each day. All of these substances are made from just a few simple building blocks called **elements.**

Elements and compounds

An element is a substance that cannot be broken down into simpler substances using chemical **reactions.** There are about 90 naturally occurring elements and a few artificial ones. About three-quarters of the elements are metals, such as magnesium and calcium, and the rest are nonmetals, such as oxygen and carbon. **Compounds** are made when elements join together in a chemical reaction. For example, magnesium and oxygen react together to make magnesium oxide, and carbon and oxygen react together to make carbon dioxide. Most of the millions of different materials in the world are compounds made up of two or more elements chemically joined together.

Atoms, protons, neutrons, and electrons

Every substance is made up of tiny particles called **atoms.** Each element contains just one type of atom, but compounds are made from two or more types of atoms joined together. Atoms are far too small to see, even with an electron microscope. Radium atoms are the largest in group 2. If you could line up them up side by side along a fifteen-centimeter (six-inch) ruler, you would need 600 million of them!

Everything you can see here, even the coral (and fish), is made from the millions of substances in the world. Most of these substances, including the water, are compounds.

Atoms themselves are made up of even smaller particles called **protons, neutrons,** and **electrons.** The protons and neutrons are found at the center of each atom in a **nucleus.** The electrons are arranged in different shells around the nucleus. Most of an atom is actually empty space—if an atom were blown up to the same size as an Olympic running track, its nucleus would be about the size of a pea! The number of the electrons in an atom and the way they are arranged in the shells determine the ways in which the element can react.

Elements and groups

Different elements react with other substances in different ways. When scientists first began to study chemical reactions, this made it difficult for them to make sense of the reactions they observed. A Russian chemist named Dimitri Mendeleev was the most successful of these. In 1869, he put each element into one of eight **groups** in a table. Each group contained elements with similar chemical properties. This made it much easier for chemists to figure out what to expect when they made elements react with each other. Mendeleev's table was so successful that the modern **periodic table** is based closely on it.

nucleus containing
protons and neutrons

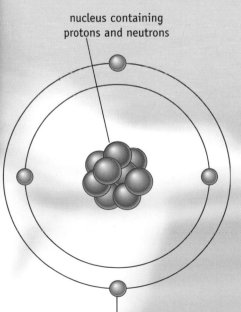

This model shows a beryllium atom. Every element has a different number of protons *(atomic number).* Each atom of beryllium contains four protons and five neutrons. Its four electrons are arranged in two shells around the nucleus.

electron

CHAPTER 2

The Periodic Table, Calcium, and the Alkaline Earth Metals

The modern **periodic table,** shown here, is based closely on Mendeleev's table. Each row in the table is called a **period,** and the **elements** in a period are arranged in order of increasing **atomic number** (number of **protons** in the **nucleus**). Each column in the table is called a **group.** Within each group, the elements have similar chemical properties to each other. For example, all the elements in group 2 are very reactive metals, and all the elements in group 18 are very unreactive gases. The elements in each group also have the same number of **electrons** in their outer shell. The elements in group 2 all have two electrons in their outer shells. It is called the periodic table because these different chemical properties occur again regularly, or periodically.

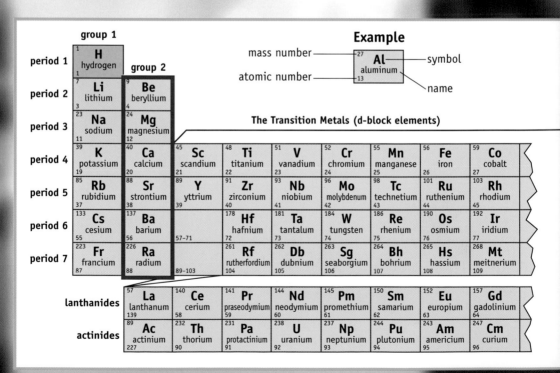

As you go down each group, the chemical properties of the elements change gradually. For example, the elements in group 2 become more **reactive** as you go down the group. Beryllium, at the top, does not react with water; calcium, in the middle, reacts quickly with water; and barium, near the bottom, reacts very vigorously with water.

Calcium and the alkaline earth metals

In this book, you are going to find out all about calcium and the other **alkaline** earth metals in group 2, as well as many of their uses.

▼ *This is the periodic table of the elements. All the elements in group 2 are metals. They are beryllium, magnesium, calcium, strontium, barium, and radium.*

Key

- metals
- metalloids
- nonmetals

group 13	group 14	group 15	group 16	group 17	group 18	
					4 **He** helium 2	period 1
11 **B** boron 5	12 **C** carbon 6	14 **N** nitrogen 7	16 **O** oxygen 8	19 **F** fluorine 9	20 **Ne** neon 10	period 2
27 **Al** aluminum 13	28 **Si** silicon 14	31 **P** phosphorus 15	32 **S** sulfur 16	35 **Cl** chlorine 17	40 **Ar** argon 18	period 3

59 **Ni** nickel 28	64 **Cu** copper 29	65 **Zn** zinc 30	70 **Ga** gallium 31	73 **Ge** germanium 32	75 **As** arsenic 33	79 **Se** selenium 34	80 **Br** bromine 35	84 **Kr** krypton 36	period 4
106 **Pd** palladium 46	108 **Ag** silver 47	112 **Cd** cadmium 48	115 **In** indium 49	119 **Sn** tin 50	122 **Sb** antimony 51	128 **Te** tellurium 52	127 **I** iodine 53	131 **Xe** xenon 54	period 5
195 **Pt** platinum 78	197 **Au** gold 79	201 **Hg** mercury 80	204 **Tl** thallium 81	207 **Pb** lead 82	209 **Bi** bismuth 83	209 **Po** polonium 84	210 **At** astatine 85	222 **Rn** radon 86	period 6
269 **Ds** darmstadtium 110	272 **Uuu** unununium 111	269 **Uub** ununbium 112		289 **Uuq** ununquadium 114		292 **Uuh** ununhexium 116			period 7

f block

159 **Tb** terbium 65	163 **Dy** dysprosium 66	165 **Ho** holmium 67	167 **Er** erbium 68	169 **Tm** thulium 69	173 **Yb** ytterbium 70	175 **Lu** lutetium 71
247 **Bk** berkelium 97	251 **Cf** californium 98	252 **Es** einsteinium 99	257 **Fm** fermium 100	258 **Md** mendelevium 101	259 **No** nobelium 102	262 **Lr** lawrencium 103

Elements of Group 2

There are six **elements** in **group** 2: beryllium, magnesium, calcium, strontium, barium, and radium. They are fairly soft, silvery-white metals that are all solids at room temperature. With the exception of beryllium, they all **react** with water to make **alkaline** solutions. This is why they are often called the alkaline earth metals.

| 9
Be
beryllium
4 | **beryllium**
symbol: Be • atomic number: 4 • metal |

The name beryllium comes from beryl, one of the **minerals** in which it is found. Emeralds are precious stones made from beryl that contains a small amount of a metal called chromium. Chromium is what gives emeralds their green color.

Beryllium is the least reactive alkaline earth metal. A very thin layer of beryllium oxide covers its surface and gives it a grey color. This layer protects the metal beneath from reacting with oxygen in the air, or with water.

Beryllium itself is **brittle,** but when mixed with other metals it produces **alloys** that are light and strong. These alloys are used in aircraft and spacecraft. Once chemists discovered beryllium, they quickly learned that its compounds have a sweet taste. However, beryllium **compounds** are very poisonous.

> *Emeralds contain beryl, a compound also known as beryllium aluminum silicate. Emeralds are green because they also contain tiny amounts of chromium and vanadium.* ▶

24	
Mg	
magnesium	
12	

magnesium
symbol: Mg • atomic number: 12 • metal

Magnesium is named after an area of Greece called Magnesia, where minerals containing magnesium are mined.

Magnesium is more reactive than beryllium, and it burns strongly with a dazzling white flame when heated in air. Because of this property, magnesium is used in flares, fireworks, and incendiary bombs (bombs that start fires instead of exploding). Magnesium alloys are used in missiles, aircraft, and drink cans. Magnesium oxide has a very high melting point and is used to make bricks for furnace linings.

Many magnesium compounds are harmful, and may irritate your eyes and throat. Others, such as magnesium hydroxide, are safe to use in medicines. Milk of magnesia, often used to cure an upset stomach, contains magnesium hydroxide powder mixed with water.

40	
Ca	
calcium	
20	

calcium
symbol: Ca • atomic number: 20 • metal

The name calcium comes from a Latin word meaning lime, or calcium oxide. It is also related to the word *chalk*—one of the many minerals that contain calcium. Calcium is also found in minerals such as limestone and marble. All of these are forms of calcium carbonate.

Calcium is more reactive than magnesium, and when heated in air, it burns with a reddish-orange flame. Calcium is an important mineral in our diet—our bones and teeth contain a lot of it, and we need to consume calcium regularly to keep these strong. Calcium oxide is used in cement and concrete, and calcium carbonate is used in making iron and steel. If you have ever broken a bone, you might have had a cast made from plaster of Paris, another name for the compound calcium sulfate.

More Elements of Group 2

88	
Sr	**strontium**
strontium	symbol: Sr • atomic number: 38 • metal
38	

Strontium is named after a town in Scotland called Strontian, where **minerals** containing strontium are mined. Strontium is more **reactive** than calcium, and it needs to be kept under oil to stop air or water from reaching it. It is so reactive that powdered strontium bursts into bright red flames on its own when exposed to air!

Strontium nitrate and strontium chlorate produce a bright red flame when burned. These **compounds** are used in tracer bullets, fireworks, and signal flares. Other strontium compounds are used to make toothpastes and the glass for color television tubes.

Isotopes are **atoms** of an **element** that have different numbers of **neutrons.** There are four natural isotopes of strontium. There are also at least twelve artificial isotopes, that are **radioactive.** The most stable radioactive isotope is strontium-90. This was released when nuclear bombs were tested above ground in the middle of the last century.

▼ *Strontium provides the red colored*
   flame in flares like this.

137	
Ba	
barium	
56	

barium

symbol: Ba • atomic number: 56 • metal

Barium is named after the Greek word for heavy. Its main **ore** is a very dense substance called barite, also known as barium sulfate.

Barium is more reactive than strontium and also needs to be kept under oil to stop air and water from reaching it. When it burns in air, barium produces a green flame.

Barium itself has very few uses, and many compounds containing barium are poisonous. Barium nitrate is very commonly used in fireworks, and barium carbonate is used as rat poison! Doctors use barium sulfate when they want to examine intestines using X-rays because this substance shows up white in X-ray images. Barium sulfate is safe to use because it does not dissolve in water, so it cannot be absorbed by our bodies.

226	
Ra	
radium	
88	

radium

symbol: Ra • atomic number: 88 • metal

Radium is a very radioactive metal that glows in the dark. It is named after the Latin word for ray. Marie Curie first discovered radium in 1898, and managed to isolate it in 1911. At the time, very little was known about **radiation.** Many researchers, including Marie Curie herself, became ill as a result of their experiments.

In the past, radium was widely used to treat cancer. Compounds such as radium chloride were used to make paints for watch dials and aircraft dials that glow in the dark. However, radium is very expensive and can cause radiation burns. As a result, it now has little practical use in our everyday lives.

CHAPTER 3

Trends in Group 2

The **alkaline** earth **elements react** with oxygen, dilute acid, and water in similar ways. Some elements are more reactive than others, however—particularly those at the bottom of the group. Beryllium, at the top of the group, is the least reactive, and radium, at the bottom, is the most reactive, although it is difficult to study its chemistry because it is both rare and **radioactive.** Gradual changes in properties like these are called trends.

Reactions with oxygen

All the alkaline earth metals react with oxygen to form metal oxides. For example, magnesium reacts with oxygen to produce magnesium oxide, MgO, and calcium reacts with oxygen to produce calcium oxide, CaO. A thin layer of metal oxide usually covers the surfaces of the alkaline earth metals. If the metal is cut or scratched, the layer is broken, and you can see the silvery metal beneath. The exposed metal reacts quickly with oxygen in the air and forms the layer of metal oxide again. This reaction is very useful because the layer of metal oxide stops the metal beneath from reacting with any more oxygen, unless it is powdered or heated.

Beryllium will react with oxygen only when it is powdered and heated. Magnesium catches fire when heated and burns with an extremely bright white light. School teachers always advise their pupils to look away from the flame because intense light can damage their eyesight without causing any warning pain. Calcium is more reactive than magnesium, but its protective layer can make it difficult to set on fire. However, if calcium is freshly cut and heated, it explodes with sparks and a reddish-orange flame!

Reactions with dilute acids

All the alkaline earth metals react with dilute acids to produce metal **salts** and hydrogen gas. Beryllium is unusual because it will also react with alkalis to produce complex beryllium salts and hydrogen. The other metals will react only with acids.

When the alkaline earth metals react with acids, they make metal salts and hydrogen (H_2). The salt made depends upon the metal and acid used. For example, if magnesium reacts with hydrochloric acid (HCl), it makes magnesium chloride ($MgCl_2$). If magnesium reacts with sulfuric acid (H_2SO_4), it makes magnesium sulfate ($MgSO_4$).

magnesium + hydrochloric → magnesium + hydrogen
acid   chloride
$$Mg(s) + 2HCl(aq) \rightarrow MgCl_2(aq) + H_2(g)$$

magnesium + sulfuric → magnesium + hydrogen
acid   sulfate
$$Mg(s) + H_2SO_4(aq) \rightarrow MgSO_4(aq) + H_2(g)$$

Magnesium ribbon reacts very quickly with acids such as hydrochloric acid. These reactions produce heat and lots of bubbles of hydrogen gas. The bubbles make the magnesium float on the surface of the acid. When magnesium reacts with hydrochloric acid, the salt produced is magnesium chloride. This dissolves quickly in the acid, causing the metal to disappear from sight. Depending upon the strength and temperature of the acid, small pieces of magnesium can vanish in a few seconds. Calcium reacts even more quickly!

◀ Magnesium ribbon burns with a brilliant white light in oxygen to make magnesium oxide. If magnesium ribbon is burned in air, some magnesium nitride is also made, because the magnesium can react with nitrogen in the air as well.

Reactions with Water in Group 2

Beryllium does not **react** with water or steam, even if it is heated very strongly. However, all the other **alkaline** earth metals react with water to produce **metal hydroxides** and hydrogen. For example, magnesium reacts with water to produce magnesium hydroxide, $Mg(OH)_2$, and calcium reacts with water to produce calcium hydroxide, $Ca(OH)_2$. These are white solids that do not dissolve particularly well in water, but do so enough to make the water alkaline.

> *When the alkaline earth metals react with water, they make metal hydroxides and hydrogen. For example, the equation for magnesium reacting with water is:*
>
> magnesium + water → magnesium hydroxide + hydrogen
> $$Mg(s) + 2H_2O(l) \rightarrow Mg(OH)_2(aq) + H_2(g)$$

Magnesium

People often expect magnesium to react violently with water because it burns so brightly in air. However, magnesium reacts very slowly with water, producing tiny bubbles of hydrogen over several days. Some of the magnesium hydroxide produced dissolves in the water, making it slightly alkaline. Although this reaction is a little disappointing, it is a different story if magnesium is heated in steam!

Magnesium burns with a blinding white light when it is heated in steam. The reaction makes a lot of hydrogen gas that can be set on fire—but only when using great care. The flame keeps burning as long as there is enough magnesium left to react with the steam. If the amount of steam used is limited, magnesium oxide is made instead of magnesium hydroxide. If a lot of steam is used in the reaction, some of it reacts with the magnesium oxide to produce magnesium hydroxide, the same **product** formed when magnesium reacts with water.

Magnesium ribbon burns in steam to make magnesium oxide and hydrogen. If the water used to make the steam contains dissolved calcium and sodium salts, the flame can be colored like this.

Calcium, strontium, and barium

Calcium is found below magnesium in the **periodic table.** It reacts with cold water far more quickly than magnesium and produces a lot of bubbles of hydrogen over just a few minutes. The water can get quite hot during the reaction, and becomes cloudy white. This is because only some of the calcium hydroxide produced dissolves in it. The rest forms a

suspension (tiny bits of undissolved calcium hydroxide mixed with the water). Strontium reacts with water more quickly than magnesium and calcium. Barium, near the bottom of the group, reacts immediately with water and produces lots of large bubbles of gas very quickly.

Dangerous alkalis

Calcium hydroxide solution and other alkalis are irritants, and must be treated carefully. If spilled on your skin, they will feel soapy. This is because they react with the oils on your skin to make soapy chemicals. They can also cause skin burns, and are particularly dangerous if they get into your eyes. When experimenting with them in the laboratory, you must always wear eye protection and take care not to get the chemicals on your skin.

Calcium reacts vigorously with water to make alkaline calcium hydroxide and bubbles of hydrogen gas.

Reasons to be Reactive

Electrons in an **atom** are arranged in shells around the **nucleus**. Chemists are usually interested in the shell farthest from the nucleus, called the outer shell. If this shell is filled completely with electrons, the atom will be unreactive. The noble gases, including helium and neon, are very unreactive because their atoms' outer electron shells are full. However, if the outer shell is not filled completely with electrons, the atom will react with other atoms to get a full outer shell. In a chemical **reaction** between a metal like magnesium and a nonmetal like chlorine, the atoms fill their outer shells by passing electrons from one to the other.

▼ *The atoms of each group 2 element get bigger as you go down the group. The two electrons in the outer shell are farther from the nucleus. These are the colors of their flames.*

Be Mg Ca Sr Ba Ra

It's all about electrons!

Atoms of nonmetals often need just one, two, or three more electrons to fill their outer shell. As a result, they get electrons from other atoms. Metal atoms are just the opposite. They have unfilled outer shells that often contain just one, two, or three electrons, and they can consequently give these electrons away to other atoms. This leaves the full electron shell beneath as the new outer shell.

None of the atoms of the **group** 2 metals have full outer shells. Instead, they have just two electrons in their outer shells. When the metals react with nonmetals, the two electrons are transferred to the nonmetal atoms. The more easily this happens, the more reactive the metal will be.

Losing electrons

Beryllium atoms are very small compared to the others in the group. The electrons in the outer shell are close to the nucleus of the atom, and are very strongly attracted to it. As a result, the electrons are difficult to lose, so beryllium is fairly unreactive. As we move down the elements of group 2, the atoms get bigger and bigger. As a result, the two electrons in the outer shell are farther and farther away from the nucleus. They become less strongly attracted to the nucleus and are lost more easily in reactions. This makes the **elements** further down the group more reactive. Radium is found at the bottom of the group. It has the largest atoms, so it is the most reactive.

The reactivity series

A list of metals in order of their reactivity is called a reactivity series. It is possible to make a large reactivity series by studying the reactions of metals other than the **alkaline** earth metals. Chemists can figure out how a metal should react with others by looking at its position in the reactivity series.

The reactivity series		
element	**group**	
potassium	1	most
sodium	1	reactive
lithium	1	
calcium	**2**	
magnesium	**2**	
aluminum	3	
zinc	transition metal	
iron	transition metal	
tin	4	
lead	4	
copper	transition metal	
silver	transition metal	
gold	transition metal	least
platinum	transition metal	reactive

The Isolation of the Alkaline Earth Metals

The **alkaline** earth metals were all discovered some years before they were isolated. Discovering an **element** can involve a process quite different from isolating it. When chemists are certain that they have found a new element, they have discovered it. However, these chemists might not be the ones who manage to isolate it. Isolation involves separating the new element from other elements to make it into a pure sample. A long time may pass before chemists manage to do this. The alkaline earth metals were not isolated until electricity was discovered.

Twitching frogs and batteries

An Italian biologist named Luigi Galvani was interested in discovering how the bodies of animals function. He was in for a bit of a shock! In 1791, he made some experiments with dead frogs and observed that they started twitching whenever he tried to pin them to an iron frame using brass pins! By accident, Galvani had discovered that muscles twitch when electricity passes through them.

Galvani thought that the electricity came from the bodies of the dead frogs, but another Italian scientist named Alessandro Volta realized that it actually came from the two different metals. He was able to use this information to make the first battery. Volta announced his new invention in 1800, and chemists rushed to test it with all sorts of chemicals to see what would happen.

Electricity and electrolysis

Within months of Volta's invention of the battery, an English chemist named William Nicholson discovered that electricity can be used to split water into its two elements, hydrogen and oxygen. When electricity is used to split up or **decompose** a **compound** into its elements, the process is called **electrolysis.**

In 1807, another English chemist named Sir Humphry Davy used electrolysis to isolate potassium metal from molten potassium hydroxide. He was so excited by his discovery that he danced around his laboratory! Davy then set out to isolate other elements from their compounds using electrolysis. In 1808, he managed to isolate magnesium, calcium, strontium, and barium. However, beryllium and radium were not isolated until some time later.

Beryllium

In 1828, the German chemist Friedrich Wöhler managed to isolate beryllium by heating beryllium chloride with potassium. Sir Humphry Davy had discovered how to isolate potassium using electrolysis 21 years earlier. Although electrolysis was not used to isolate beryllium, it was needed to make the potassium that Wöhler used when he isolated beryllium.

Radium

Radium was discovered much later than the other alkaline earth metals, and was not isolated until 1911. Once again, the metal was isolated using electrolysis. The Polish-French chemist Marie Curie not only helped discover radium, but she also later isolated it.

This replica shows one of Volta's batteries. It used disks made from two different metals, such as zinc and copper or zinc and silver. The disks were separated by paper soaked in salty water or acid, and stacked in a glass tube. A pile of twenty or more pairs of metal disks could deliver quite a painful electric shock.

CHAPTER 4

Beryllium

Beryllium is a very hard, **brittle,** gray metal. A thin layer of beryllium oxide covers its surface, protecting the metal from **reacting** with water or steam, even when strongly heated. However, beryllium will react with oxygen if heated to about 1,112 °F (600 °C). Beryllium's original name was glucinium, meaning sweet. It was called this because its **compounds** have a sweet taste. Unfortunately, they are also very poisonous and can cause skin rashes.

Dust containing beryllium and its compounds can cause a lung disease called berylliosis. The lungs of sufferers become swollen and inflamed, and the people find it difficult to breathe. We are unlikely to be exposed to beryllium in our everyday lives, but beryllium and its compounds are important industrial hazards and must be handled very carefully.

The discovery and isolation of beryllium

A French chemist named Louis Vauquelin discovered beryllium in 1798. He studied some crystals of beryl and emerald that were sent to him by René Haüy, a fellow Frenchman who believed that substances with identical crystals must also be chemically identical. Beryl and emerald crystals are very similar, and Vauquelin was able to show that they did contain the same chemical. He was also able to show that they contained a new **element,** beryllium. However, he was unable to isolate it. The French chemist Antoine-Alexandre-Brutus Bussy and the German chemist Friedrich Wöhler both isolated beryllium by heating mixtures of potassium and beryllium chloride in 1828.

Aquamarine is a precious stone containing beryl. It is blue because it contains small amounts of iron. There is a myth that says it is the mermaid's treasure and that it keeps sailors safe at sea. ▶

The equation for the reaction Bussy and Wöhler used is:

beryllium + potassium chloride $\xrightarrow{\text{heat}}$ beryllium + potassium chloride

$$BeCl_2(s) + 2K(s) \rightarrow Be(s) + 2KCl(s)$$

*The reaction happens because potassium is higher up in the reactivity series than beryllium and is able to **displace** beryllium from beryllium chloride. The potassium chloride produced dissolves easily in water, leaving solid beryllium.*

Extraction of beryllium

Beryllium is found in about 30 **minerals,** including beryl and the precious stones emerald and aquamarine. Beryl is a compound called beryllium aluminum silicate, that contains beryllium, aluminum, silicon, and oxygen. It is the most important industrial source of beryllium. About 280 tons of it are mined each year, two-thirds of it in the United States.

The **extraction** of beryllium from beryl happens in two stages. In the first stage, beryl is heated strongly with a compound called sodium hexafluorosilicate to produce beryllium fluoride. In the second stage, the beryllium fluoride is mixed with magnesium and heated to around 1,652 °F (900 °C). This reaction produces beryllium and magnesium fluoride.

The equation for the second stage in beryllium extraction is:

beryllium + magnesium fluoride $\xrightarrow{\text{heat}}$ beryllium + magnesium fluoride

$$BeF_2(s) + Mg(s) \rightarrow Be(s) + MgF_2(s)$$

The reaction happens because magnesium is higher up in the reactivity series than beryllium, so it is able to displace beryllium from beryllium fluoride.

Uses of Beryllium

Beryllium is more resistant to bending than steel, but it is less dense than aluminum. It also has a high melting point compared to other light metals. It can be mixed with other metals to make lots of different **alloys,** and it has some interesting properties that allow it to be used in nuclear reactors and X-ray machines.

Beryllium metal

Beryllium is used to make parts for aircraft and spacecraft that must be both light and strong. It is used in high-speed aircraft and satellites—the space shuttles contain window frames and supporting beams made from the metal. Beryllium conducts heat well and it has a high heat capacity. This means that it can absorb a lot of heat energy without becoming as hot as other metals. It is so efficient that it is used in the brakes of the space shuttles. These produce tremendous amounts of heat, because a shuttle is very heavy and touches down much faster than a normal aircraft.

Windows and moderators

Beryllium has some useful nuclear properties. It is not transparent to ordinary light, but does allow X-rays to pass through it easily. As a result, it is used in the windows of X-ray machines and **radiation** detectors.

The heart of a nuclear power station is its reactor core, where **atoms** of metals such as uranium break apart and release energy. When a high-speed **neutron** hits a uranium atom, the atom splits into two. When it does so, it releases some energy and three more neutrons. These neutrons then go on to split more uranium atoms. This process, called a chain reaction, produces the heat energy in the reactor. The speed of the neutrons is very important in these chain reactions. Beryllium is used to slow down any neutrons traveling too fast to split the uranium atoms. Substances like beryllium that can do this are called moderators.

▲ Lightweight beryllium alloys are used in engine components and in guidance and sensor systems of military helicopters.

Beryllium alloys

Copper is a very good conductor of electricity, but alloys of beryllium and copper are much tougher. They are used to make electrical contacts in mobile phones and computers, and special tools that do not cause sparks when they are used. These are particularly useful in dusty factories where a stray spark could cause an explosion. Beryllium-aluminum alloys are lighter and stiffer than aluminum alone, and are used in the manufacture of satellites, helicopters, golf clubs, bicycle frames, and any object that requires a low weight.

Beryllium compounds

Beryllium chloride is used as a **catalyst** in the chemical industry to speed up reactions. Beryllium oxide is an insulator used in electrical circuits and car electronic ignition systems. It is also used in the armor for army tanks, and in microwave ovens and gyroscopes. Green crystals of beryllium aluminum silicate are cut to shape and sold as gemstones. They are, of course, known more commonly as emeralds.

CHAPTER 5

Magnesium

Magnesium is a soft, silvery-white metal. It has a low **density** (lower than that of beryllium), making pieces of magnesium feel light for their size. It is usually too weak to be used on its own, so it is mixed with other **elements** to produce light but strong **alloys.** A thin layer of magnesium oxide covers its surface, protecting the metal from **reacting** with air or water unless it is heated strongly. However, magnesium reacts rapidly with acids even when cold. Molten magnesium must be protected from the oxygen in air by gases such as sulfur dioxide.

The discovery and isolation of magnesium

In 1755, a Scottish chemist named Joseph Black discovered magnesium while studying the reactions of magnesium and calcium **compounds.** Black studied magnesia, now known as magnesium oxide, and lime, now known as calcium oxide. At the time, chemists did not know which elements were in these compounds, but Black was able to show that substances made from magnesia were different from those made from lime. When he reacted magnesia with sulfuric acid, he made a **salt** that dissolved in water. A similar experiment using lime produced a salt that did not dissolve in water. From his experiments, Black knew that magnesia contained a different metal from the metal in lime, but he could not isolate it. Magnesium was not isolated until electricity was discovered.

In 1808, Sir Humphry Davy isolated magnesium by passing electricity through a mixture of molten magnesium oxide and mercury oxide. For his **electrolysis** experiments, Davy built the world's largest battery, with 2,000 pairs of metal disks!

▲ The experiments of Joseph Black (1728–1799) with magnesium and calcium compounds led him to discover magnesium, although he was unable to isolate it.

Extraction of magnesium

Magnesium is the eighth most abundant element in Earth's crust, making up about 2.5 percent of it. **Minerals** such as dolomite and magnesite contain magnesium compounds, but magnesium is never found naturally as a free metal. Each cubic meter (264 gallons) of seawater has more than 2.9 lb (1.3 kg) of magnesium dissolved in it. Thus, most magnesium is **extracted** from seawater rather than from minerals.

In the first stage of the extraction process, calcium oxide is added to seawater, causing solid magnesium hydroxide to form. This is collected and reacted with hydrochloric acid to make magnesium chloride, $MgCl_2$.

The equation for the production of magnesium chloride is:

magnesium + hydrochloric → magnesium + water
hydroxide   acid   chloride

$$Mg(OH)2(aq) + 2HCl(aq) \rightarrow MgCl2(aq) + 2H2O(l)$$

In the second stage, the magnesium chloride is melted and electricity is passed through it. Magnesium is produced at the negative electrodes and floats to the top of the molten magnesium chloride. Chlorine gas is produced at the positive electrodes. It is collected and used to make more hydrochloric acid for the first stage.

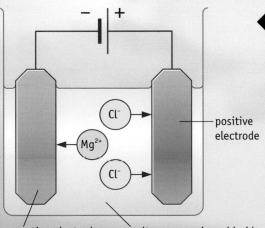

negative electrode   molten magnesium chloride

◀ *In the production of magnesium by electrolysis, the molten magnesium chloride contains electrically charged particles called* **ions.** *The magnesium ions are positively charged and are attracted to the negative electrode, where they become magnesium* **atoms.**

Uses of Magnesium

Magnesium is quite high in the reactivity series, so it is able to **displace** less reactive **elements** from their **compounds**. This is very useful in metal production and rust prevention. Magnesium can be mixed with other metals to produce lightweight **alloys.**

Metal production

The final stage in producing uranium metal from its **ore** is called the Ames process. Uranium tetrafluoride is mixed with lots of powdered magnesium and heated in a special container. The **reaction** gives out so much heat that the temperature goes up to more than 2,372 °F (1,300 °C), melting the magnesium fluoride slag and producing uranium. The slag floats on top of the uranium and is removed when the container is cooled down again.

The equation for the reaction in the Ames process is:

magnesium   +   uranium   →   magnesium + uranium
tetrafluoride   fluoride

$$2Mg(s) + UF_4(s) \rightarrow 2MgF_2(s) + U(s)$$

The reaction happens because magnesium is higher up in the reactivity series than uranium, so it is able to displace uranium from uranium tetrafluoride.

Steel is iron that contains less than 2 percent carbon, with other elements added to it to improve its properties. Some elements, such as sulfur, must be removed from the steel while it is being made. To do this, magnesium powder is blown into the molten steel. Magnesium is more reactive than iron and removes the sulfur from it, forming a magnesium sulfide slag. This floats on the molten steel and is scraped off.

Sacrificial protection

Iron and steel objects corrode and become rusty when they are exposed to oxygen and water. To stop them from rusting, they are usually painted, oiled, or coated in plastic.

However, this is not always easy to do, and paint can chip or flake off, leaving the metal exposed. Another method to prevent rust, called sacrificial protection, is used for large ships, pipelines, and oil rigs. A large bar of magnesium is bolted on to the object or connected to it with a cable. Because magnesium is more reactive than iron, it corrodes instead of the steel. As long as the magnesium stays in contact with the steel, all the steel is protected. However, the magnesium is gradually eaten away and has to be replaced every so often. This process is still easier than trying to paint a large object in difficult places.

Magnesium alloys

Magnesium has a low **density,** and as a result, objects made from it are light for their size. Unfortunately, magnesium is relatively weak compared to other metals and is usually mixed with other metals to make alloys. Duralumin is a lightweight but strong alloy discovered early in the 20th century by Alfred Wilm. It is mostly aluminum, with about 4 percent copper, between 0.5 percent and 1.5 percent magnesium, and some manganese. Duralumin is easily worked into shape, but becomes much harder and stronger when treated with heat. It is widely used in aircraft, spacecraft, cars, and other machinery.

▲ Most commercially produced magnesium metal is extracted from seawater. Magnesium alloys are lightweight and are extremely useful in the aerospace industry.

Magnesium Compounds

Magnesium reacts vigorously with oxygen when heated in air, producing a blinding white light. This **reaction** is used in distress flares, fireworks, and in some types of flash photography. The magnesium oxide produced is one of several very useful magnesium **compounds.**

Magnesia bricks

The biggest single use for magnesium compounds is in refractory bricks—special bricks that are used to line the inside of blast furnaces, ovens, and kilns. The best ones, called magnesia bricks, contain magnesium oxide. This has a very high melting point, 5,165.6 °F (2,852 °C), so it is very useful for making refractory bricks. Magnesite **ore** (magnesium carbonate) is heated strongly to make periclase (magnesium oxide), that is then made into bricks. Without these refractory bricks, blast furnaces would melt when being used!

▲
Eight-inch (20-centimeter) thick steel blocks are reheated until nearly molten. This furnace is lined with magnesium oxide refractory bricks to deal with the heat.

Milk of magnesia

Your stomach contains hydrochloric acid. This is needed to kill harmful bacteria that might be in your food, and it provides the acidic conditions needed to digest proteins. However, you can get indigestion if your stomach produces too much acid. Antacids are medicines that help to cure the indigestion by reacting with the extra acid. One antacid is called milk of magnesia. It is a thick white suspension of magnesium hydroxide in water. When you swallow some, it reacts with some of the hydrochloric acid, making you feel better.

The equation for the reaction of magnesium hydroxide with hydrochloric acid is:

magnesium + hydrochloric → magnesium + water
hydroxide   acid   chloride

$$Mg(OH)_2(aq) + 2HCl(aq) \rightarrow MgCl_2(aq) + 2H_2O(l)$$

Magnesium hydroxide is also used as a flame retardant—a chemicals that makes it more difficult to set material or plastic on fire. When it is heated, magnesium hydroxide takes in heat energy and breaks down to release water vapor. This reaction helps to keep the plastic cool for longer in a fire.

A dose of Epsom salt

Magnesium sulfate is often called Epsom **salt.** It gets its name from the **mineral** water at Epsom in England, where magnesium sulfate occurs naturally in a mineral called epsomite. Commercial quantities of Epsom salt are made by reacting magnesium carbonate with sulfuric acid. The salt has many uses, including cement and **fertilizer** manufacture, cosmetic lotions, bath salts, fireproofing, and the "snow" in films. Large doses of magnesium salts can cause diarrhea, but when used carefully, Epsom salt works as a traditional laxative that can help if you are constipated.

Magnesium chloride

Magnesium chloride is a drying agent. It is added to foods such as canned vegetables to help keep them firm. It is also used to remove snow and ice from roads in the winter. When salts such as magnesium chloride are mixed with ice, they lower its melting point. Magnesium chloride melts ice even as low as 5 °F (−15 °C), and does less damage to plants and concrete than other salts, such as sodium chloride. However, roads treated with it can become slippery if no snow falls, since it absorbs moisture from the air.

◀ Epsom salt is used to reduce swelling and help bruises. It is also used in the dyeing of some textiles and in leather tanning.

Magnesium and Life

Cattle and sheep can develop a condition called "grass tetany" or "grass staggers" if they do not get enough magnesium in their diet. This makes it difficult for the animals to control their movements. They twitch and stagger about, and they can die in severe cases. Adding magnesium chloride to their food can prevent this illness. Magnesium is important to living things in a number of other ways.

Magnesium in the body

Magnesium is an important **mineral** in our diet because it plays a vital part in the chemistry of our cells. **Enzymes** are biological **catalysts** that are made from proteins, and many of them need "cofactors" to work properly. Cofactors are metal **ions**—metal **atoms** that have lost **electrons** from their outer shells. Magnesium ions (Mg^{2+}) are cofactors for enzymes that control the release of energy by our cells. Without magnesium, our nerves and muscles would not work properly. This is why animals suffer from the "staggers" if they do not get enough magnesium in their diet. Our recommended daily allowance for magnesium is 350 mg, but magnesium deficiency is rare because green vegetables contain a lot of it.

Magnesium ions play a vital part in keeping the DNA in our cells in its helical shape.

Chlorophyll

Green plants can make their own food in a process called **photosynthesis.** They use the energy from light to **react** carbon dioxide and water together, making glucose and oxygen.

The equation for photosynthesis is:

$$\text{carbon dioxide + water} \xrightarrow{\text{light}} \text{glucose + oxygen}$$
$$6CO_2(g) + 6H_2O(1) \longrightarrow C_6H_{12}O_6(aq) + 6O_2(g)$$

Photosynthesis can happen in plant cells because they contain tiny objects called chloroplasts. Animal cells do not contain chloroplasts, so animals cannot make their own food. Chloroplasts contain a green protein called chlorophyll, that absorbs the light needed for photosynthesis. The world's plants make about 300 tons of chlorophyll per second, making it one of the most abundant proteins on Earth. At the heart of each chlorophyll **molecule** there is a magnesium ion.

The magnesium ion is vital for chlorophyll to work. If it is removed, the chlorophyll turns brownish-green and cannot absorb light properly. This is unlikely to happen in a living plant, but it can happen when green vegetables are cooked.

Chlorophyll in vegetables

Green vegetables lose their color if they are cooked too long, because the chlorophyll gets washed out. They can also turn brownish-green if they are cooked in slightly acidic water. This is because the remaining chlorophyll molecules lose their magnesium ions, causing them to change their color. To stop this from happening, some cooks add sodium hydrogencarbonate to the cooking water. It becomes slightly **alkaline,** allowing the magnesium ions to stay in the chlorophyll molecules. However, part of the chlorophyll molecule itself is lost this time, giving it an olive green color. The vegetables look more appetizing, but the alkali speeds up the **oxidation** of vitamin C in the food, and some of the nutritional values is lost.

CHAPTER 6

Calcium

Calcium is a hard, silvery-white metal, but granules of it look dull gray because a thin layer of calcium oxide covers the surface. It **reacts** rapidly with cold water and acids, and it reacts violently with air when it is heated. Pure calcium has few industrial uses. However, **compounds** that contain calcium, particularly calcium carbonate and calcium oxide, are widely used in the manufacture of iron and steel, glass, and cement. Our bones and teeth contain calcium, and calcium is an important **mineral** in our diet.

The discovery and isolation of calcium

Calcium is the fifth most abundant element in Earth's crust, making up about 3.6 percent of it. Calcium compounds are found in many minerals, such as calcium carbonate in limestone, chalk, and marble; calcium sulfate in gypsum; and calcium phosphate in phosphate rock. Calcium compounds have been in use for thousands of years. For instance, the Romans used calcium carbonate to make calcium oxide, which they used to mix concrete. However, calcium is not found naturally as a free metal. It was not isolated until 1808, when Sir Humphry Davy passed electricity through a mixture of molten calcium oxide and mercury oxide.

Extraction of calcium

The raw material for calcium production is calcium chloride, a by-product of the sodium carbonate industry. It can also be made by reacting hydrochloric acid with calcium carbonate from shells and rocks such as limestone. The calcium chloride is melted, and then electricity is passed through it. This causes calcium to form at the negative electrode and chlorine gas to form at the positive electrode.

Pieces of calcium react rapidly with the air and rarely look shiny like this. ▶

Uses of calcium

Calcium is high up in the reactivity series, so it can remove oxygen from the oxides of less reactive metals. For example, it is used to **extract** uranium from uranium oxide and chromium from chromium oxides. In the same way, calcium is also used to remove oxygen and sulfur from metal **alloys.**

Calcium has proved to be useful as a chemical that absorbs gases to maintain or improve the vacuum in a vacuum tube. Vacuum tubes are electronic components used in some specialized devices, including radio and television transmitters. As much air as possible must be removed from them during manufacture so that they perform well.

Small amounts of calcium metal are mixed with other metals such as aluminum and magnesium to produce alloys with useful properties. For example, lead is a soft metal, but it becomes much harder when even a very small amount of calcium is added to it. Lead-calcium alloys are used in bearings in machinery and to protect telephone cables from damage. Lead-calcium alloys containing about 0.1 percent calcium are used in the lead plates found in car batteries. This is because they last longer and need less maintenance than plates made from other materials, such as lead-antimony alloy.

chalk

marble

limestone

▲ *Limestone, chalk, and marble are all forms of calcium carbonate.*

Calcium Carbonate

Calcium carbonate is a solid **compound** of calcium, carbon, and oxygen. Living things in the oceans, such as snails and crabs, use carbon dioxide dissolved in the water to make calcium carbonate for their shells. Huge numbers of microscopic animals and plants called plankton also make their shells from calcium carbonate. When these living things die, they sink to the seabed and form layers of shells. The layers, called sediments, build up on top of each other. Their weight squeezes the water out from between the shells, and they become stuck together by salt crystals. In this way, sedimentary rocks called limestone and chalk are formed over thousands of years. They can be nearly pure calcium carbonate.

▲ *These white chalk cliffs are in the south of England. The Latin word for chalk is* creta, *and the Cretaceous Period (144 to 66 million years ago) is named after the huge chalk deposits laid down during this time.*

Limestone

Limestone is a tough rock widely used for buildings, walls, and paving stones. It contains crystals of calcium carbonate, varying in size from ones that are large enough to see, to microscopic crystals only 0.001 millimeter (0.000039 inch) across. Limestone often also contains fossils of dead animals and plants that were trapped in the sediments as the rock formed. Crushed limestone is used in road building, and powdered limestone can be used to **neutralize** the acid in acidic lakes and rivers. Some limestones contain phosphates, so they are used to make **fertilizers.** One of the biggest uses of limestone is as a source of calcium oxide, a compound that is used extensively in industry.

Chalk

Chalk is a white crumbly rock made almost entirely from microscopic shells. This makes it much softer than limestone. Builders use a piece of string rubbed in chalk to make straight lines on the ground and on building materials. Pool players rub chalk on the end of their cue sticks, and gymnasts and weightlifters rub it into their hands to get a better grip. Chalk can be ground up to make a very fine powder called whiting. Putty is made from whiting mixed with a little linseed oil, and it is used to fill holes in woodwork and to seal glass into windows. Whiting is also used in crayons, rubber, paints, and cosmetics. The chalk used by teachers to write on a chalkboard is not actually made from chalk, but from another calcium compound called calcium sulfate. Chalk is one of the raw materials used in the manufacture of cement and some fertilizers.

Marble

If limestone or chalk becomes buried deep underground by earth movements, they are put under pressure and heated without melting. Their crystal structure changes to form a metamorphic rock called marble. Marble is shiny, and is harder than limestone or chalk. It can be polished to an attractive finish, so it is used for statues, for kitchen and bathroom countertops, and as a decorative surface on buildings. Marble comes in different colors, but the most valuable form is white (statuary) marble. Sculptors use this to create statues and sculptures.

This is the Taj Mahal in northern India. It is over 70 meters (230 feet) high and was built from marble in the 17th century by more than 20,000 workers.

Limestone and Limewater

When calcium oxide is added to water, it forms a solution of calcium hydroxide. This is often called limewater, and it is used to test for carbon dioxide gas. When calcium hydroxide and carbon dioxide **react** with each other, a cloudy white suspension of calcium carbonate forms in the limewater.

The equation for the limewater test is:

calcium + carbon → calcium + water
hydroxide dioxide   carbonate

$$Ca(OH)_2(aq) + CO_2(g) \rightarrow CaCO_3(s) + H2O(l)$$

This test is used to see if carbon dioxide is produced by a chemical reaction, and to show that living things produce carbon dioxide when they respire.

The limewater eventually becomes clear if more carbon dioxide is bubbled in. This is because a weak acid called carbonic acid forms. It reacts with the calcium carbonate to make calcium hydrogencarbonate, that dissolves in water.

The equation for the reaction between calcium carbonate and carbonic acid is:

calcium + carbonic →   calcium
carbonate   acid   hydrogencarbonate

$$CaCO3(s) + H2CO3(aq) \rightarrow Ca(HCO3)2(aq)$$

This reaction can cause huge caves to form, buildings to disintegrate, and water to become hard form dissolved salts.

Acid attack!

If you put a drop of hydrochloric acid onto a piece of limestone, chalk, or marble, the rock fizzes and begins to disappear. This is because the calcium carbonate in the rock reacts with the acid. Rain is naturally acidic because carbon dioxide dissolves in it to make carbonic acid. Although this is a weak acid, rain and rivers that contain carbonic acid react with deposits of limestone and chalk. Over thousands of years, vast underground caves and channels can form in the rock.

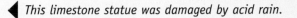
This limestone statue was damaged by acid rain.

Fossil fuels such as coal and oil often contain sulfur. When these fuels are burned, sulfur dioxide gas is produced. It then dissolves in the clouds to form acid rain. In very badly polluted places, the rain can be more acidic than lemon juice! If acid rain falls on buildings, statues, and other stonework made from limestone, it attacks the stone and wears it away.

Stalactites and stalagmites

When water containing calcium hydrogencarbonate drips from the roof of caves, it evaporates to leave columns of solid calcium carbonate behind. These are called stalactites and stalagmites. Stalactites hang down from the ceiling, and stalagmites grow up from the floor. Sometimes they meet and form strange shapes—some legends claim these are the remains of witches!

The equation for the production of a stalactite or stalagmite from a solution of calcium hydrogencarbonate is:

$$\text{calcium hydrogencarbonate} \rightarrow \text{calcium carbonate} + \text{water} + \text{carbon dioxide}$$

$$Ca(HCO_3)_2(aq) \rightarrow CaCO_3(s) + H_2O(l) + CO_2(g)$$

Solid calcium carbonate is left behind when the water evaporates and the carbon dioxide escapes into the atmosphere.

Spectacular stalactites and stalagmites can be seen in Mitchell Caverns in California's Mojave National Scenic Area.

Calcium, Hard Water, and Health

It is usually easy to make soap lather in soft water. However, if it is very difficult to get soap to lather, your water is hard. This does not mean that it is really tough, but that it contains dissolved magnesium and calcium **salts.** These get into the water if it flows over rocks such as limestone, chalk, gypsum, or dolomite. The salts react with the fatty acids in soap, making a sticky gray-white scum that makes it difficult to get you and your clothes clean. Even modern soapless detergents need higher temperatures and more detergent to get clothes clean than they do in soft water.

Hard water

Salts such as calcium sulfate cause permanent hardness. It is called permanent hardness because the water stays hard when it is boiled. Salts such as calcium hydrogencarbonate cause temporary hardness. It is called temporary hardness because the water becomes soft when it is boiled. This happens because the calcium hydrogencarbonate breaks down to form solid calcium carbonate. Unfortunately, this calcium carbonate builds up a spiky white "scale" that damages kettles and irons. The scale that builds up inside boilers and hot water pipes can help to stop them from corroding. However, if it gets too thick, the pipes can become so clogged that they have to be replaced. Kettles and irons can be "descaled" by using acids to keep them working properly.

▼ *It is difficult to form a lather in hard water. Instead, a sticky scum forms. But soap easily forms a lather in soft water.*

Softening water

Sodium carbonate, also called washing soda, can soften water. It does this by reacting with the calcium salts to form solid calcium carbonate that does not interfere with soap. Washing powders often contain chemicals called phosphates. These stop the calcium salts in the water from reacting with soap, improving the performance of the washing powder. Some homes in hard water areas may have **ion** exchangers plumbed into their water supply. An ion exchanger contains special beads that can trade sodium ions for calcium ions. As the water passes through, calcium ions from the dissolved calcium **compounds** stick to the beads. Sodium ions come off of them and dissolve in the water. Ion exchangers need to be recharged every so often by passing some salty water through them.

Healthy hard water?

The dissolved salts in hard water give it a pleasant taste. Calcium is an important mineral in our diet, and hard water helps to supply it. Calcium is needed for our blood to clot properly, for our muscles and nerves to work properly, and for maintaining healthy teeth and bones. There is also some evidence that people living in hard water areas suffer fewer heart attacks than those living in areas with soft water.

Water is an important part of ▶ *our diet, and we should drink at least 2.1 quarts (2 liters) a day. Hard water also contains calcium salts that help to keep our teeth and bones healthy.*

Bones

Without a skeleton, we would be floppy and would look very different. The skeleton does many important jobs, including supporting the body, giving it a shape, and allowing the muscles to move it. It also protects vital organs inside, such as the lungs and brain. Our skeleton, called an endoskeleton because it is inside our body, is made from bone. There is about 2.2 lb (1 kg) of calcium in a typical 154-lb (70-kg) person, and about 99 percent of this is stored in the bones.

Strong but flexible

Bones need to be strong enough to carry the weight of a body without being squashed or bent. Cells called osteoblasts inside the bone produce crystals of a hard **mineral** called hydroxylapatite. This is a type of calcium phosphate that makes up over half the weight of the bone. Bones must also be flexible to prevent them from snapping easily when bent or pulled. Bones get their flexibility from a tough elastic protein inside them called collagen. Bones are made from a "composite material"—they contain two different types of material and get the best out of both. Hydroxylapatite is strong when squashed but easily snapped, while collagen is strong when stretched or bent, but easily squashed.

▼ The top chicken bone was heated in an oven for half an hour, leaving the minerals behind, and the one below was soaked in vinegar overnight to dissolve out the minerals. The bone from the oven snaps easily, but the one soaked in vinegar is soft and floppy.

Astronauts and old age

Calcium is constantly moving in and out of our bones, depending on our diet and on how we use our bodies. Osteoblasts produce hydroxylapatite, but other cells called osteoclasts remove it. Bone builds up in places where more hydroxylapatite is produced than is removed. This usually happens in bone put under pressure from exercise. Bone becomes weaker where more hydroxylapatite is removed than is produced. This usually happens in bone that is not put under pressure—for example, through lack of exercise. It is natural for bone to change like this throughout our life.

Astronauts in space are weightless, so their bones are not under pressure. Their bones quickly lose hydroxylapatite, limiting how long astronauts can spend in space. As we get older, hydroxylapatite is eventually lost from our bones faster than it is replaced. This is part of the natural aging process, but some old people lose so much hydroxylapatite that they get osteoporosis. Their bones become weak and easily broken, and they become shorter and bent over.

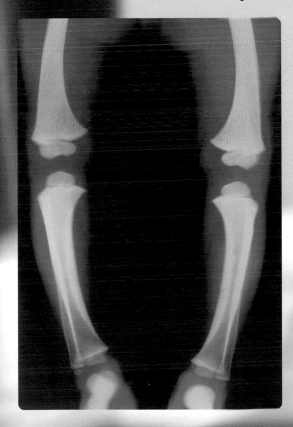

Eat well and exercise

Calcium is an important mineral in our diet. It is found in foods such as milk, cheese, and tofu. If we do not get enough calcium in our diet, we run the risk of getting weak bones and teeth (which also contain calcium). Vitamin D is important for controlling the levels of calcium and phosphorus in our bodies. Children who do not get enough vitamin D can develop rickets, causing their legs to become curved. Eggs, butter, and margarine are good sources of vitamin D, and our bodies can also make it when we play outside in the sunshine.

◄ *This X-ray shows the bowed legs of a child suffering from rickets.*

Calcium Oxide

If calcium carbonate is heated strongly, it **decomposes** to form calcium oxide and carbon dioxide. Calcium oxide is also called lime or quicklime. It is a base, meaning that it can **react** with acids and **neutralize** them. Farmers may spread calcium oxide on their fields to neutralize excess acid in the soil, but it has many other uses in industry.

The equation for the decomposition of calcium carbonate is:

$$\text{calcium carbonate} \xrightarrow{\text{heat}} \text{calcium oxide} + \text{carbon dioxide}$$
$$CaCO3(s) \rightarrow CaO(s) + CO2(g)$$

Iron and blast furnaces

Iron is **extracted** from iron **ore** in a huge steel column called a blast furnace. This is lined with heat-resistant bricks to stop it from melting in the heat. The raw materials needed are iron ore, coke, and limestone. Hot air is blasted into the bottom of the furnace to burn the coke, eventually producing carbon monoxide. This reacts with the iron ore to make molten iron. However, the molten iron contains sandy impurities from the original iron ore. These must be removed from the iron by a process using limestone.

Calcium oxide gives off ▶ *very bright limelight when it is heated by the flame from a mixture of oxygen and hydrogen.*

In the heat of the blast furnace, the limestone decomposes to form calcium oxide and carbon dioxide. The calcium oxide reacts with the sandy impurities to make a molten slag. This floats on the surface of the iron, and is easily removed to leave purified iron behind.

The equation for the production of slag in a blast furnace is:

calcium oxide + silicon dioxide → calcium silicate
$$CaO(s) + SiO_2(s) \rightarrow CaSiO_3(l)$$

Sand is mostly silica, or silicon dioxide. This reacts with the calcium oxide from the limestone to produce a calcium silicate slag.

Cooled and solidified slag can be used in building roads. Glassy granules are made if the slag is cooled very quickly with jets of water. These granules are ground to a fine powder that can be used in the manufacture of strong, fire-resistant concrete.

Cement and concrete

When heated, the calcium carbonate in chalk breaks down to produce calcium oxide and carbon dioxide. Cement is made by strongly heating a mixture of chalk and clay. If cement, sand, aggregate (small stones), and water are mixed together, concrete is made. Enough concrete is used around the world to provide everyone on the planet with a ton each year! Mortar (used by builders to join bricks together to make walls) is made by mixing calcium oxide with sand and water.

Making glass

Glass can be made by melting sand, then cooling it very quickly. Sand melts at 3,092 °F (1,700 °C). To reduce the energy needed to create this much heat, glass manufacturers add sodium carbonate. This breaks down in the heat to form sodium oxide, reducing the melting temperature to 1,472 °F (800 °C). Unfortunately, it makes glass that dissolves in water! To prevent this, calcium carbonate is also added, forming calcium oxide in the glass. About 90 percent of glass is this soda-lime glass or bottle glass.

More Calcium Compounds

Coal-fired power stations, and some industries, produce sulfur dioxide gas as a by-product. This gas will cause acid rain if it is allowed to escape into the atmosphere. One method to stop it from escaping uses powdered calcium oxide. This reacts with the sulfur dioxide to produce a **compound** called calcium sulfate, used in toothpaste and lipstick. Blackboard chalk is really calcium sulfate and not chalk at all.

The equation for removing sulfur dioxide using calcium oxide is:

calcium + sulfur + oxygen → calcium
oxide   dioxide   sulfate

$$2CaO(s) + 2SO_2(g) + O_2(g) \rightarrow 2CaSO_4(s)$$

Gypsum and plaster of Paris

Gypsum is a sedimentary rock that contains calcium sulfate, $CaSO_4$. Powdered gypsum is used widely for plaster and plasterboard to line walls and ceilings in buildings. The crystals of calcium sulfate in gypsum contain a small amount of water. Plaster of Paris is made by heating gypsum to 212 °F (100 °C) to remove the water from it. When water is added back to plaster of Paris, it warms slightly, expands, and then sets hard. Dentists use it to make casts of teeth, and artists use it to make molds for their works of art. Forensic scientists use plaster of Paris to make a permanent record of shoe or tire prints left behind at the scene of a crime. Plaster of Paris casts are also used to hold broken bones still while they mend.

▲ *Dentists use plaster of Paris when making molds of their patients' teeth.*

Fertilizers and flames

Plants need **minerals** to grow properly, especially nitrogen, phosphorus, and potassium. Artificial **fertilizers** are often added to the soil to provide these minerals. Phosphate rock contains calcium phosphate. This would make a good source of phosphorus for plants, but it does not dissolve in water. As a result, plants cannot absorb it through their roots, so fertilizer manufacturers convert it to ammonium phosphate, a compound that does dissolve in water.

Calcium carbide, CaC_2, is a manufactured gray solid that reacts vigorously with water. The **reaction** produces calcium hydroxide, $Ca(OH)_2$, and acetylene, C_2H_2. Acetylene is a very flammable gas that is used as the fuel in oxyacetylene **welding** and cutting torches, because it produces a very hot flame.

Calcium chloride

Calcium chloride, $CaCl_2$, is a useful waste **product** from the sodium carbonate industry. It absorbs moisture, so the oil industry uses calcium chloride to dry oil fractions, and chemists use it in their experiments if they want to remove moisture from the air. It is also used as a food additive—it absorbs water and keeps the food firm.

Calcium chloride is used to remove snow and ice from roads in the winter. When **salts** such as calcium chloride are mixed with ice, they lower the melting point of the ice, causing it to melt. Calcium chloride works particularly well, right down to -23.8 °F (–31 °C), because heat is released when it dissolves in water.

◀ *Grit and calcium chloride are spread on roads to prevent ice and snow from building up in winter.*

CHAPTER 7

Strontium

Strontium is a soft, silvery-white metal. When exposed to the air, it **reacts** quickly with oxygen to form a layer of yellowish strontium oxide, SrO. To prevent it from doing this, strontium is usually stored under oil, just like the **group** 1 metals. Strontium carbonate is used widely in the manufacture of glass for television tubes but, in general, strontium **compounds** have few industrial uses. This is because their properties are very similar to those of compounds containing calcium or barium, but they are more expensive.

The discovery and isolation of strontium

Adair Crawford and William Cruickshank discovered strontium in 1790 when they studied a **mineral** from a lead mine near Strontian in Scotland. At first they thought that the mineral was witherite, which contains barium carbonate, but they were able to show that it was quite different. They called the new mineral strontianite, which we now know contains strontium carbonate. Crawford and Cruickshank knew that strontianite contained a new metal, but they could not isolate it. Sir Humphry Davy managed to isolate strontium eighteen years later by passing electricity through a mixture of molten strontium chloride and mercury oxide.

▲ These crystals are celestite, or strontium sulfate. Celestite is used to make strontium nitrate, which provides the red color in fireworks and tracer bullets.

Extraction of strontium

Strontium is quite rare in Earth's crust, making up about 0.045 percent of it. Minerals such as strontianite and celestite (strontium sulfate) contain strontium, but it is never found naturally as a free metal. About half a million tons of strontium minerals are mined in the world each year, mostly in China, Mexico, and Spain. Very little strontium metal is made commercially because it is very similar to calcium and barium, which are more widely available. Strontium is **extracted** by the **electrolysis** of a mixture of molten strontium chloride and potassium chloride. When electricity is passed through the mixture, strontium metal forms at the negative electrode and chlorine gas forms at the positive electrode.

Uses of strontium

More than three-quarters of the strontium produced is used to make glass for cathode ray tubes. These are used in televisions and computer monitors, and they produce small amounts of X-rays as part of their normal operation. Strontium carbonate, $SrCO_3$, is added to the molten glass while it is being made. It breaks down in the heat to produce carbon dioxide and strontium oxide. The strontium oxide absorbs X-rays when the cathode ray tube is used. Flat panel displays and cathode ray tubes work differently, so the demand for strontium is likely to go down as flat displays become more popular.

Strontium hydroxide, $Sr(OH)_2$, reacts with fatty acids from oils to make substances called metallic soaps. These do not dissolve easily in water, and are used in the manufacture of thick, waterproof greases. Strontium chloride, $SrCl_2$, or strontium acetate, $Sr(CH_3COO)_2$, are the active ingredients in toothpastes for sensitive teeth. Tiny liquid-filled holes in the teeth, called tubules, can connect to nerves. This can make teeth sensitive to hot drinks and cold foods. The strontium compounds block these tubules, reducing the sensitivity of the teeth.

Strontium carbonate is used in the manufacture of glass for television sets and computer monitors. As wide-screen televisions become more popular, the demand for strontium is likely to go up.

Radioactive Strontium

In the middle of the last century, nuclear weapons were tested above ground. These "atmospheric tests" produced a lot of **radioactive** fallout that contained dangerous radioactive **isotopes.** These were carried around the world by the wind and found their way into the water and soil. One of the more dangerous radioactive isotopes was strontium-90.

Isotopes

Isotopes are **atoms** of an **element** that have the same number of **protons** and **electrons,** but different numbers of **neutrons.** There are four natural isotopes of strontium, but strontium-88 is the most abundant or common. It makes up 82.6 percent of natural strontium. It has 38 protons and 50 neutrons in its **nucleus,** and it is given the chemical symbol ^{88}Sr.

Radiation

The atoms of the four natural strontium isotopes are stable, meaning that they do not break up into smaller pieces. However, the atoms of some isotopes are unstable, so they can break up or **decay** into smaller pieces. When they do this, they may become another isotope of the same element, or an isotope of another element. They also give out **radiation.**

There are different types of radiation. Depending on the type of radiation produced, it can pass through the air, plastic, and metal, and into our bodies. If radiation damages the DNA in our cells, it can lead to cancer. To prevent this, there are strict laws to protect us from overexposure to radioactive chemicals. Strontium-90 (^{90}Sr) emits powerful **beta radiation,** consisting of fast-moving electrons fired out of the nucleus as it decays.

Half-life

Nobody can predict when an individual atom will decay. However, if scientists study huge numbers of atoms, they can say how long it would take for half of them to decay. The time it takes for half of the atoms to decay is called the

half-life of the isotope. Some stable isotopes have half-lives of thousands or millions of years, but some unstable isotopes have half-lives of only a fraction of a second. Strontium-90 is the most stable artificial isotope of strontium, with a half-life of 28.1 years. It is an artificial isotope because it is made in nuclear **reactions** and does not occur naturally.

▼ *Different types of radiation can go through different types of materials. **Alpha radiation** is stopped by paper; beta radiation is stopped by sheets of aluminum; and **gamma radiation** is stopped by very thick sheets of lead.*

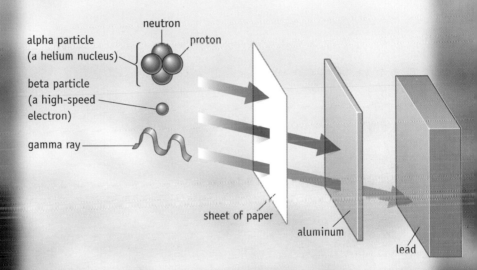

neutron

alpha particle
(a helium nucleus)

proton

beta particle
(a high-speed electron)

gamma ray

sheet of paper

aluminum

lead

Strontium-90

Strontium and calcium are chemically very similar, and the cells of plants and animals cannot easily tell them apart. This means that plants and animals absorb strontium, which can be dangerous if some of it is strontium-90 from nuclear fallout. If strontium-90 contaminates food, such as milk, it can become concentrated in bones and teeth, where its radiation may cause leukemia and bone cancer.

Strontium-90 is not all bad, though. It can be used in some luminous signs. Heat is produced as it decays, and this can be converted into electricity in a nuclear battery. These batteries are used to supply electricity over a long period of time in difficult places such as weather stations in remote areas, navigation buoys at sea, and space probes.

CHAPTER 8

Barium

Barium is a soft, silvery-white metal that is slightly harder than lead. When barium is exposed to the air, it quickly **reacts** with oxygen to form a layer of barium oxide. To prevent it from doing this, it is usually stored under oil or in an unreactive atmosphere such as argon gas. Barium metal has very few uses, and many barium **compounds** are poisonous—barium carbonate is used as rat poison. Chemists use barium chloride to detect sulfates in chemicals, and barium nitrate is used to produce an apple green flame for fireworks and signal flares.

The discovery and isolation of barium

In 1774, Swedish chemist Carl Scheele discovered barium when he studied a **mineral** called pyrolusite. Scheele was able to show that this contained a new compound, which we now know is barium oxide. He was unable to isolate the metal, but he managed to make barium sulfate crystals by reacting the barium oxide with sulfuric acid. He sent some of the crystals to his friend Johan Gahn, a fellow Swede. In 1775, Gahn showed that a mineral called barite contained barium sulfate, but he could not isolate barium either.

Sir Humphry Davy managed to isolate barium in 1808 when he passed electricity through a mixture of molten barium oxide and mercury oxide. He named the metal barium, from the Greek word for "heavy." This was because minerals containing barium, such as barite, have a high **density** compared to many other minerals. However, barium itself has quite a low density, just a third more than aluminum. Some chemists complained about the name, but it became too late to change

These crystals are white barite, or barium ▶
*sulfate. Barite is the main **ore** of barium.*
It is used in special X-rays as barium
meals and enemas. It is also used in oil,
paper, and rubber industries.

it.

Extraction of barium

Barium is quite rare in Earth's crust, making up about 0.04 percent of it. Barium is never found naturally as a free metal, but it is contained in minerals like witherite (barium carbonate) and barite. Over two million tons of these minerals are mined in the world each year, mostly in the United States, Denmark, and France. Like the other **alkaline** earth metals, barium is **extracted** by **electrolysis.** When electricity is passed through molten barium chloride, barium metal forms at the negative electrode and chlorine gas forms at the positive electrode.

Uses of barium

Barium is a very reactive metal, so barium and **alloys** of barium and aluminum are used to remove traces of gases such as oxygen from vacuum tubes. These are electronic components used in some specialized devices, and they will not work if they contain even small amounts of gas.

The equation for barium removing oxygen from a vacuum tube is:

$$\text{barium} + \text{oxygen} \rightarrow \text{barium oxide}$$
$$2Ba(s) + O_2(g) \rightarrow 2BaO(s)$$

A tiny amount of solid barium oxide is formed.

Barium-nickel alloys give off **electrons** easily when they are heated. They are used in spark plugs to ignite the fuel in car engines, and in the cathode ray tubes used for television sets and computer monitors.

Barium Compounds

Chemists sometimes need to find out if a liquid contains dissolved sulfates. To do this, they add a few drops of barium chloride, $BaCl_2$, solution to the liquid. If there are any sulfates in the liquid, they form barium sulfate, $BaSO_4$. This is a white solid that does not dissolve in water, so the mixture turns cloudy white. Barium sulfate and other barium **compounds** are useful in industry, too.

One equation for the test for a sulfate is:

$$\text{sodium} + \text{barium} \rightarrow \text{sodium} + \text{barium}$$
$$\text{sulfate} \quad \text{chloride} \quad \text{chloride} \quad \text{sulfate}$$
$$NaSO_4(aq) + BaCl_2(aq) \rightarrow 2NaCl(aq) + BaSO_4(s)$$

In this example, sodium sulfate is detected. Barium sulfate does not dissolve in water and forms a white **precipitate.** A few drops of hydrochloric acid are usually added as well, to stop other barium compounds from forming and spoiling the result.

Paint and barium meals

Barite is a **mineral** that contains barium sulfate. Powdered barite is often used as a **filler** in the manufacture of rubber, plastics, and paper. Fillers are substances added to materials to make them cheaper or stiffer. It can also be mixed with mud to make a dense liquid called slurry. This is used to lubricate the cutting bits used to drill oil wells.

White paint used to contain lead carbonate, which is poisonous. An alternative called lithopone was developed near the end of the 19th century. To make it, barium sulfate and zinc sulfide are mixed together and heated strongly for a long time. Lithopone was widely used as the white pigment in paints and face powder. However, it has largely been replaced by titanium dioxide, which is cheaper.

X-rays do not pass though barium easily, so barium sulfate mixed with water is used in X-ray examinations of the

This barium X-ray shows a healthy small intestine. In the past, surgeons would have had to operate in order to see what was happening in the body. Today X-rays like this help them to diagnose first.

stomach and intestines. If the patient swallows the mixture, it is called a "barium meal," and if it is passed into his or her rectum through a tube, it is called a "barium enema." When the radiologist takes an X-ray photograph of the patient, the stomach or intestines show up white wherever the barium sulfate has gone. Barium sulfate is not absorbed through the intestines, and it leaves the body when the patient goes to the toilet.

Glass and rat poison

The cathode ray tubes used in television sets produce small amounts of X-rays as part of their normal operation. Barium oxide, BaO, can be added to the glass to absorb the X-rays. When the glass is being made, it is mixed with barium carbonate, $BaCO_3$. This breaks down in the heat to produce carbon dioxide and the required barium oxide.

Barium carbonate is used in rat poison. It is not poisonous immediately because, like barium sulfate, it does not dissolve in water. However, once it is in the rat's stomach, the barium carbonate reacts with the hydrochloric acid there to form barium chloride. This does dissolve in water and passes through the rat's intestines to poison it. The same would happen to a human, so it should be avoided.

CHAPTER 9

Radium

Radium is a rare, silvery-white metal. It is the most **reactive alkaline** earth metal. Not only does it react with oxygen in the air to form radium oxide, RaO, it reacts rapidly with nitrogen to form a black coating of radium nitride, Ra_3N_2. Radium is intensely **radioactive** and glows in the dark, but it has no practical applications in our everyday lives. In the last century, however, radium had many uses. It was used to make luminous paints for watch dials, and in cancer treatments. It was even used in some very strange potions sold by people posing as doctors until the dangers of **radiation** were fully understood.

The discovery and isolation of radium

Marie Curie was a Polish-French scientist who was born in 1867. While studying uranium and its **ore**, pitchblende, she discovered that the pitchblende was more radioactive than the uranium itself. She realized that there had to be other **elements** in the pitchblende that were more radioactive than uranium. Marie set out to isolate these elements from pitchblende with help from her husband, Pierre. In 1898, they managed to produce two tiny fractions of intensely radioactive material. One fraction contained an element that they called polonium, after Poland, where Marie was born. The other fraction contained another element that was even more radioactive than polonium. They called it radium, after the Latin word for ray.

Later, Marie Curie and André Debierne tried to isolate some radium from a ton of pitchblende. By 1910, they had managed to **extract** about 0.0035 oz (0.1 gram) of radium. They used **electrolysis** to do this, just as Humphry Davy had done with the other **alkaline** earth metals over a hundred years earlier.

Marie and Pierre Curie work in their laboratory in 1903. ▶

▲ *This is a sample of uranium ore called pitchblende. The yellow orange areas are uranium hydroxide (gummite), and the darker areas are uranium oxide (uraninite). Pitchblende contains tiny amounts of uranium.*

Extraction of radium

Radium is formed only by the radioactive **decay** of other elements, such as uranium, so it is rarely found in Earth's crust. However, it is concentrated in uranium ores, such as pitchblende and carnotite from the United States, Canada, Australia, and Zaire. Even so, one ton of ore can produce as little as 0.0053 oz (0.15 g) of radium, and only about 3.53 oz (100 g) of radium is produced each year. Because radium is very chemically reactive, it is usually supplied as radium chloride, $RaCl_2$, or radium bromide, $RaBr_2$. These **compounds** are more stable chemically than the metal itself, which is extracted from radium chloride by electrolysis if it is needed.

Radium and radioactivity

Radium is about two million times more radioactive than uranium, and all its uses rely on its intense radioactivity. There are over 30 radium **isotopes,** with **half-life** ranges from 1,600 years for radium-226 to less than two millionths of a second for radium-217. The modern unit of radioactivity is the becquerel (Bq), or one radioactive decay per second. But the old unit of radioactivity was the curie, the same amount of radioactivity as in 0.035 oz (1 g) of radium-226 (equal to 37 billion becquerel).

Uses of Radium

Radium gives off powerful **radiation** as it **decays.** The dangers of this were not known when radium was discovered. Marie Curie was fascinated by the way her laboratory glassware glowed in the dark at night because of the traces of radium on it, and Pierre Curie used to carry radium around in his waistcoat pocket. The radiation caused a large sore patch on his chest, but it did not kill him—a heavy horse-drawn cart did that in 1906. Marie Curie died of leukemia in 1934, most probably caused by exposure to radiation.

Radiation and cancer treatment

Although exposure to radium may cause cancer, the radiation can be used to kill cancer cells if it is carefully controlled. Radium was widely used in the last century for radiotherapy, the treatment of cancer using radiation. Marie Curie herself worked very hard to research radium and to promote its use in radiotherapy. In 1920 she started the Curie Foundation to raise money for the Radium Institute in Paris. During a tour of the United States a year later, the president presented her with a gram (0.035 oz) of radium. To pay for it, the American Association of University Women had raised $156,413—then an enormous amount of money. The gift doubled the amount of radium the Institute had to use for its scientific and medical research! However, modern radiotherapy uses cheaper and safer sources, such as cobalt-60.

Luminous dials

Zinc sulfide glows in the dark, but a mixture of zinc sulfide and radium glows even more brightly. It was this mixture that was first used in luminous paints. Although radium was very expensive, very little was needed because it is so radioactive. As a result, in the early part of the last century, all sorts of objects were painted with radium paints, including the hands of watches, instrument dials, and even buttons. Unfortunately, the women who applied the paint in factories suffered from the effects of radiation, and many of them became ill with cancer. As a result, radium is no longer used for luminous paints.

Amazing but true!

Despite the growing understanding at the start of the last century about the dangers of radiation, all sorts of strange products containing radium were sold to an eager and unsuspecting public during the 1920s and 1930s. As it decays, radium produces radon gas. Radon was believed to improve health and kill germs, among other claims, and people thought that radium would be even more effective. **Radioactive** water containing radium was very fashionable as a beverage. People even made their own radioactive water using containers lined with radioactive **minerals.** Bandages and pads containing radium were popular treatments to ease the joint pain of rheumatism and arthritis, and other products containing radium included soap, toothpaste, and skin creams! Inevitably, many people fell seriously ill, and the craze for radium ended. Modern products like these do not contain radium, and must be tested rigorously to avoid any risks to health.

CRÈME
SCIENTIFIQUE

CURATIVE
EMBELLISSANTE

THO-RADIA
à base de thorium et de radium selon la formule du
DOCTEUR ALFRED CURIE
EN VENTE EXCLUSIVEMENT CHEZ LES PHARMACIENS

◀ *This 1933 advertisement is for a facial cream containing radium and thorium. Even scientists were unaware of how dangerous these substances were. One year later, Marie Curie died from leukemia from her work with radioactive **elements**.*

Find out More About the Alkaline Earth Metals

Elements
The table below contains some information about the properties of the **alkaline** earth metals.

Element	Symbol	Atomic number	Melting point °F/°C	Boiling point °F/°C
beryllium	Be	4	2,348.6/1,287	4,478.2/2,469
magnesium	Mg	12	1,202/650	1,994/1,090
calcium	Ca	20	1,547.6/842	2,703.2/1,484
strontium	Sr	38	1,430.6/777	2,519.6/1,382
barium	Ba	56	1,340.6/727	3,398/1,870
radium	Ra	88	1,292/700	3,158.6/1,737

Compounds
These tables show you the chemical formulas of most of the **compounds** mentioned in the book. For example, calcium carbonate has the formula $CaCO_3$. This means it is made from one calcium **atom,** one carbon atom and three oxygen atoms, joined together by chemical **bonds.** Nearly all these compounds are solid at room temperature.

Barium compounds

Barium compound	formula
barium carbonate	$BaCO_3$
barium chlorate	$Ba(ClO)_2$
barium chloride	$BaCl_2$
barium nitrate	$Ba(NO_3)_2$
barium oxide	BaO
barium sulfate	$BaSO_4$

Beryllium compounds

Beryllium compound	formula
beryllium aluminum silicate	$Be_3Al_2(SiO_3)_6$
beryllium chloride	$BeCl_2$
beryllium fluoride	BeF_2
beryllium oxide	BeO

Calcium compound	formula
calcium carbide	CaC_2
calcium carbonate	$CaCO_3$
calcium chloride	$CaCl_2$
calcium hydrogencarbonate	$Ca(HCO_3)_2$
calcium hydroxide	$Ca(OH)_2$
calcium hydroxyphosphate	$Ca_{10}(PO_4)_6(OH)_2$
calcium hypochlorite	$Ca(ClO)_2$
calcium nitride	Ca_3N_2
calcium oxide	CaO
calcium phosphate	$Ca_3(PO_4)_2$
calcium silicate	$CaSiO_3$
calcium sulfate	$CaSO_4$
hydroxylapatite	$Ca_{10}(PO_4)_6(OH)_2$

Magnesium compound	formula
magnesium carbonate	$MgCO_3$
magnesium chloride	$MgCl_2$
magnesium fluoride	MgF_2
magnesium hydroxide	$Mg(OH)_2$
magnesium nitrate	$Mg(NO_3)_2$
magnesium oxide	MgO
magnesium sulfate	$MgSO_4$
magnesium sulfide	MgS

Radium compound	formula
radium bromide	$RaBr_2$
radium chloride	$RaCl_2$
carnotite	$K_2(UO_2)_2V_2O_8$
pitchblende	UO_2 and UO_3

Find out More (continued)

Acids

Acid	formula
phosphoric acid	H_3PO_4
sulfuric acid	H_2SO_4
vitamin C (ascorbic acid)	$C_6H_8O_6$

Strontium compounds

Strontium compound	formula
strontium carbonate	$SrCO_3$
strontium chloride	$SrCl_2$
strontium acetate	$Sr(CH_3COO)_2$
strontium hydroxide	$Sr(OH)_2$
strontium nitrate	$Sr(NO_3)_2$
strontium oxide	SrO
strontium sulfate	$SrSO_4$

Other compounds

Compound	formula
carbon dioxide (gas)	CO_2
copper nitrate	$Cu(NO_3)_2$
acetylene (gas)	C_2H_2
mercury oxide	HgO
potassium chloride	KCl
potassium hydroxide	KOH
silicon dioxide	SiO_2
sodium carbonate	Na_2CO_3
sodium chloride	$NaCl$
sodium hexafluorosilicate	Na_2SiF_6
sodium hydrogencarbonate	$NaHCO_3$
uranium tetrafluoride	UF_4
water (liquid)	H_2O

Glossary

alkaline having a pH above 7. When a base such as calcium hydroxide dissolves in water, it makes an alkaline solution.

alloy mixture of two or more metals, or mixture of a metal and a nonmetal

alpha radiation (α radiation) waves of energy caused by quickly moving helium nuclei that have broken away from an unstable nucleus

atom smallest particle of an element that has the properties of that element

atomic number number of protons in the nucleus of an atom

beta radiation (β radiation) waves of energy consisting of fast-moving electrons produced by an unstable nucleus when it breaks up

bond force that joins atoms together

brittle likely to break into small pieces when hit

catalyst substance that speeds up reactions without getting used up

compound substance made from the atoms of two or more elements, joined together by chemical bonds

decay process in which the nucleus of a radioactive substance breaks up, giving off radiation and becoming the nucleus of another element

decomposition type of chemical reaction in which a compound breaks down into simpler substances, such as the elements that make it up

density mass of a substance compared to its volume (how much space it takes up). To find the density of a substance, you divide its mass by its volume. Substances with a high density feel very heavy for their size.

displace to take the place of something else, as when one element takes the place of another in a compound

electrolysis process of breaking down or decomposing a compound by passing electricity through it. The compound must be molten or dissolved in a liquid for electrolysis to work.

electron particle in an atom that has a negative electric charge. Electrons are found in shells around the nucleus of an atom.

element substance made from only one type of atom

enzyme substance made by living things that controls the chemical reactions that happen in it

extract to remove a chemical from a mixture of chemicals

fertilizer chemical that gives plants the elements they need for healthy growth

filler substance added to a product to make it cheaper or to improve its properties

gamma radiation (γ radiation) powerful waves of energy caused by very high frequency light waves. Gamma radiation cannot be seen, and it can pass through metal.

group vertical column of elements in the periodic table. Elements in a group have similar properties.

half-life time taken for half the atoms of a radioactive substance to decay

ion charged particle made when atoms lose or gain electrons. If an atom loses electrons, it becomes a positive ion. If an atom gains electrons, it becomes a negative ion.

isotope atoms of an element with the same number of protons and electrons, but a different number of neutrons. Isotopes share the same atomic number but they have a different mass number.

mass number the number of protons added to the number of neutrons in an atom's nucleus

metal hydroxide compound containing metal ions and hydroxide ions (OH^-)

mineral substance that is found naturally in the earth but does not come from animals or plants. Metal ores and limestone are examples of minerals.

molecule smallest particle of an element or compound that exists by itself. A molecule is made from two or more atoms joined together.

neutralization reaction between an acid and an alkali or a base. The solution made is neutral, meaning that it is not acidic or alkaline.

neutron particle in an atom's nucleus that has no electric charge

nucleus central part of an atom made from protons and neutrons. It has a positive electric charge.

ore substance containing minerals from which metal can be taken out and purified

oxidation adding oxygen to, or removing electrons from, an element or compound in a chemical reaction. For example, carbon is oxidized when it reacts with oxygen to make carbon dioxide.

period horizontal row of elements in the periodic table

periodic table chart in which all the known elements are arranged into groups and periods

photosynthesis chemical reaction in which green plants make sugars from carbon dioxide and water, using the energy from light. Oxygen is also made.

precipitate solid that appears when two solutions are mixed

product substance made in a chemical reaction

proton particle in an atom's nucleus that has a positive electric charge

radiation energy or particles given off when an atom decays

radioactive producing radiation

reaction chemical change that produces new substances

salt compound formed when an acid is neutralized by a base

subatomic particle particle smaller than an atom, such as a proton, neutron, or electron

welding joining two or more metals together, usually by heating them

Timeline

calcium and magnesium discovered	1755	Joseph Black
barium discovered	1774	Carl Scheele
strontium discovered	1790	Adair Crawford and William Cruickshank
calcium isolated	1808	Sir Humphry Davy
barium isolated	1808	Sir Humphry Davy
strontium isolated	1808	Sir Humphry Davy
magnesium isolated	1808	Sir Humphry Davy
beryllium isolated	1828	Antoine-Alexandre-Brutus Bussy and Friedrich Wöhler
radium discovered	1898	Marie Curie and Pierre Curie
radium isolated	1910	Marie Curie and André Debierne

Further reading and Useful Websites

Books

Fullick, Ann. *Science Topics: Chemicals in Action*. Chicago: Heinemann Library, 1999.

Oxlade, Chris. *Chemicals in Action* series, particularly *Atoms, Elements, and Compounds*. Chicago: Heinemann Library, 2002.

Websites

WebElements™
http://www.webelements.com
An interactive periodic table crammed with information and photographs.

DiscoverySchool
http://school.discovery.com/students
Help for science projects and homework, and free science clip art.

Proton Don
http://www.funbrain.com/periodic
The fun periodic table quiz!

Creative Chemistry
http://www.creative-chemistry.org.uk
An interactive chemistry site with fun practical activities, quizzes, puzzles, and more.

Mineralogy Database
http://www.webmineral.com
Lots of useful information about minerals, including color photographs and information about their chemistry.

Index

7/64

mL